Passing the Harp

Four Celtic Allegories

Passing the Harp

Four Celtic Allegories

David Cole

ANAMCHARA BOOKS

Passing the Harp:
Four Celtic Allegories

Anamchara Books
Vestal, NY 13850
www.anamcharabooks.com

Paperback ISBN: 978-1-62524-276-1

Author: David Cole.

Contents

Introduction

Storytelling has long been a part of our humanity. Ever since we could communicate we have in all likelihood been telling stories to one another; certainly for thousands of years, stories have been told and collected, orally and through writing. Stories help us to make sense of the world. Through them, we begin to fathom who we are, where we have come from, and where we might go from here. They enable us to learn from our past so that we can better step into the future. They allow us to be inspired by people who came before us through hero sagas and true-life accounts.

Many of the greatest spiritual teachers through the ages have used storytelling as a way of getting across truths so deep they may be impossible to put in words. Jesus used allegory and illustrations from real life to express and expand his message. Known as the "Parable," these stories still communicate to a part of our minds that is deeper than our rational intellect.

The ancient Celts, like many cultures, loved stories. The eighth-century historian Bede tells us in his *Ecclesiastical History of the English People* of the ancient Celtic tradition called "Passing of the Harp," where communities would gather in the Mead Hall, or other communal hall, and tell stories through the evenings around a fire, with food and drink flowing. This tradition was continued in the Celtic monastic communities, such as the one in Whitby, where Bede makes mention of it. The first storyteller in the English language, Cædmon, brought to life Bible stories and told them in the common language of the ordinary folk. Accounts of saints' lives were also popular among the early Celtic Christians. These stories show what the Almighty Intimate Creator of all things can do through ordinary people who allow the Divine Spirit to move in and through them.

This is what storytelling is all about: connecting deep truths with ordinary lives to make those lives extraordinary. The medium of storytelling may have changed over the years from the oral tradition with the passing of the harp to written stories in books to movies and television programs, and now in various digital formats—but the stories themselves are as important to our culture as ever. Storytelling is within our DNA, a part of who we are as human beings.

The stories included in this collection are a few short allegorical tales intended to help readers gain a deeper sense of peace within themselves amid life's struggles, a sharper awareness of the joys to be experienced in a life lived in the Divine flow. At the end of each story, I have included a reflection and meditation to encourage deeper thought. I hope these stories will linger with you, unfolding themselves as they're needed, until they are transformed into a practical reality within your life.

The first tale, "Skellig and the Standing Stone," was adapted from an ancient Celtic tale. It tells of a man whom God tells to do something seemingly nonsensical. The man allows the voice of another to dissuade him from his calling. Subtly, this intruder puts a misrepresentation onto what God has said, and so discourages the man from doing what God has called him to do, making him believe it is a foolish and impossible task. The story is a reminder that God works all things for good (Romans 8:28) in ways that we may not be able to see except with hindsight.

The second tale, "Ashes and Ravens," is an adaptation of a story by Jenifer Rees Larcombe who runs a Christian healing organisation called Beauty from Ashes. She described my retelling as "a wonderful story" which is "just great," and I know she doesn't mind me including it here. It tells of a girl who has a terrible life and loses everything she held dear (and some things that she did not). In desperation she turns to the local king for help, only to find that he has been watching over her all along. The girl and the king create something beautiful out of what seemed to be destruction and devastation in the girl's life. (You can learn more about Jenifer and Beauty from Ashes at http://beautyfromashes.co.uk.)

The third tale, "Bags of Stones," was inspired by a story by Randy Alcorn, as well as by Revelation 22:12, where Jesus promises to return, bringing with him a "reward" for each of us, according to how we have lived our lives. The story is about the journey of life—and about how the journey continues on after what we might call "death," which is not an end but simply a transference of our existence. We live in one way in one place, and that determines where and how we live "beyond the Garden wall." Companions and guides travel through life with us, and how we respond to them is important. How we act towards those around us and all that happens in life has an effect on who we are, and this has an effect that lasts longer than the realm where we currently live. (To learn more about Randy Alcorn's perspectives on eternity, go to http://www.epm.org.)

The fourth and final tale, "Parable of the Prisoner," is completely original. It reflects on what I have found, in my pastoral and counselling ministry, to be a very common scenario: when we are freed by the power of God from the chains and bondage of our false selves, many of us do not really live in the fullness of that freedom. Instead, we often choose to live in the memory of the past, believing that we are not actually free. Listening to lies whispered in our ears, we create for ourselves imaginary prisons we think are real.

Please take these tales and read them to yourself—but don't stop there! Read them out loud to others; share them with friends and with gatherings of people. Stories shouldn't be kept between the book and your eyes, or between the writer and the reader. By their very nature, stories are meant to be shared. That's part of their wonder.

May your own story be enriched by these and many other stories. And may you never lose the love of good stories, nor the desire to tell them to others.

David Cole.

Summer 2015

Sacred storytelling is a pilgrimage—
a pilgrimage to a place called Hope.
Andy Fraenkel

1
Skellig and
the Standing Stone

There was once a man named Skellig who lived alone in a house on a mountain that overlooked a village. His land was vast and wild, kept for the creatures to find shelter. Often he would walk about alone speaking out loud to God, as if God was walking right there beside him.

One day Skellig opened the door of his house to go for a walk and there before him, at the threshold of his home, stood God himself.

"Walk with me," said God. "I have something for you to do."

Skellig walked with God away from his home along paths he knew well, and where he had often spoken to God as he walked. This time, however, he was silent, simply walking beside God. God led him into a nearby meadow within the boundary of

Skellig's land. In the centre of the meadow was a huge standing stone, three times as high as Skellig stood and twice as wide as his height. Skellig had often come to this place, knowing that it was a "thin place," a place where the membrane between the worlds was very slight.

Skellig and God stood looking at the huge standing stone.

"For an hour every morning and an hour every evening," God said, "I want you to push against this standing stone."

Skellig looked at the standing stone and then turned to look back at God, but God was no longer there. So Skellig stared at the stone for a while longer with the words of God ringing in his ears and heart. Then slowly he turned and walked back to his home, again in silence, contemplating the meaning of God's words.

Skellig was obedient to God, and so for an hour every morning and an hour every evening Skellig left his home and pushed against the standing stone.

The days passed into weeks, which passed into months, and for an hour every morning and an hour every evening Skellig left his home and pushed against the standing stone.

One day, as Skellig was pushing against the stone, a traveller passed by and sat under the nearby oak tree.

"I am Dern," said the traveller. "May I ask what you are doing?"

"I am Skellig," replied Skellig, "and I am pushing against this standing stone."

Dern sat silently watching for a while, and then with a smirk he said, "Why are you pushing against the standing stone?"

"Because God told me to," replied Skellig.

"Oh . . . ," said Dern. "What for?"

Skellig could not answer, since he had not questioned God. He had never wondered why; he just knew God had told him to do it, so he did.

Undeterred by Dern, for an hour every morning and an hour every evening Skellig continued to leave his home and push against the standing stone. Often, Dern would appear a little after Skellig began his task. Each time, Dern would sit under the tree and watch Skellig pushing with all his might against the stone. Whenever Skellig glanced at Dern, he always wore that same smirk across his face as he sat in the shade of the oak tree.

After several days, Dern said, "It's no use you know, pushing against the standing stone. You will never push it over. You will never even move it."

Skellig ignored Dern's words for many days, but now every time Skellig came to push against the standing stone, Dern was there, doing his best to discourage him by telling him that it was no use pushing against the stone as he would never move it or push it over.

Finally, one day, Dern's words settled in Skellig's mind. On the walk back to his home, his thoughts turned from God to the words of Dern. Skellig started to doubt what he was doing, until one morning as he opened the door of his house to go to the standing stone, he decided not to go after all. He would stay and get some extra work done in his house instead.

A week later, Skellig needed to go to the village for supplies. That morning, as he stepped out of his door, there, sitting to one side, was God.

"What are you doing here?" asked God.

"I am going to get supplies from the village," replied Skellig.

God looked straight into Skellig's eyes. "You should be at the standing stone."

Skellig turned to God and anger burned inside him. "Why did you send me to push against the standing stone when you knew I would not be able to move it? Why did you ask me to do something that you knew I would not be able to do? Why did you ask me to do something knowing I would fail? I will never be able to push that standing stone over! Why did you waste my time?"

"Who said that I wanted you to push the stone over?" asked God. "Wherever did you get the idea that I wanted you to move the standing stone? Don't you think that if I wanted it moved I could have picked it up and moved it myself?"

Skellig thought for a moment and then looked at God in puzzlement.

"Look at your arms and your legs," said God. "Look at the muscles you have gained by pushing against the standing stone. Now come, the time I have been preparing you for is at hand."

At this, God stood up and walked off down the mountainside toward the village. Skellig felt ashamed of himself for doubting God and having his anger burn within him. Quietly, he set off, following God.

In the centre of the village ran a wide river with a fast and violent current. The villagers had built a wooden bridge over the river, as the town buildings stood on one side and their homes stood on the other.

God led Skellig down to the banks of the river and under the bridge. "Stay here," God said. "The time I have been preparing you for is at hand."

Skellig looked at the river and up at the bridge that stood above him. He turned to look back at God, but God was no longer there.

Skellig waited under the bridge at the riverside. The day passed and the sun began to set. Suddenly, Skellig heard a familiar voice,

"What are you doing down there?"

Skellig looked up at Dern, who was standing above him at the end of the bridge.

"I am waiting," said Skellig.

"Waiting?" asked Dern. "For what?"

This question Skellig could not answer, as once again he had not questioned God.

"Come with me," said Dern gently. "We shall go into town and enjoy the evening. Don't waste your time here any longer. The tavern is warm and its food is wonderful!"

But Skellig did not listen to Dern. He remembered the feeling that had sank within him as God spoke to him earlier, asking why he had not been at the standing stone. Although Dern continued to try to persuade Skellig to come away with him, Skellig stayed where he was until Dern went away alone.

Skellig went back to waiting. Soon, he heard the sound of children running from the town side of the river, coming home after school. All the children, about a hundred in all, ran onto the bridge.

Just then Skellig heard an almighty sound. A great rock had been ripped out from the riverbed by the current and was being thrown downstream. The rock hit the legs of the bridge at the far side of the river. The legs buckled—and the bridge started to collapse. The children, now all in the centre of the bridge, screamed. They huddled together as the opposite end of the bridge fell into the river and was washed away.

The bridge above Skellig's head then began to break away. As quickly as he could move, he lifted his hands to the bridge and held it in place until all the children had run across. When all the children were safely off the bridge, Skellig let the bridge go. It crashed into the river and was washed away in the current, dashing against rocks and breaking into pieces.

Skellig heard the sound of cheering from the villagers. The villagers declared Skellig a hero, a strong man who had been smart enough to be in the right place at the right time. Skellig knew that he was only able to hold up the bridge because of the strength he had built from pushing against the standing stone. Only his obedience to God had made him strong—and only obedience to God had put him under the bridge when his strength was needed most.

Reflection

Often in our lives we may feel we are led by some form of Divine interaction to do something. We may use the phrase "called," or we may say something is our "calling." We don't walk and talk with a visible God as Skellig does, but nevertheless there is an unmistakable tugging within us toward a particular course of action.

Sometimes, perhaps oftentimes, this sense of calling makes little sense. We may feel we have been called to do something impossible. We may wonder if we are simply wasting our time, if our energies might be spent somewhere else far more productively.

But if we trust that God has a plan, then we follow this sense of silent direction. As it says in Proverbs

20:24, "The Lord directs our steps, so why try to under-stand everything along the way?" (NLT). Somethings are simply beyond our rational intellects' abilities to understand.

However, we sometimes think that anything we can't understand isn't true. (Of course, if this were the case, then most of us would think that television and the Internet were mere flights of fancy—and quantum physics would clearly consist of delusions and lies!) In other words, "Dern" shows up. He can take many forms. Often he speaks loudest when he uses the voice of our own self-doubts: "I'm not good enough"; "I can't do this"; "Why am I even bothering?" (Psychol-ogists call this negative self-talk, and they know how powerfully our thoughts can hold us back.) "Dern" may also use the voices of others, even people who love us and wish us well, asking us to second guess our actions, to see them as silly and pointless.

Sometimes, the lie we hear is just a little twist of a truth, which causes us to think twice. In Skellig's case, Dern was absolutely correct—Skellig was never going to move the standing stone. Dern is sly and subtle enough to make Skellig get angry and frustrated. But God never asked Skellig to move the rock, just to push against it.

MEDITATION

What do you believe God has called you to?

It may not be something you consider big or important, but in reality every small action is important in the Divine Cosmic Plan. It could be parenting your children . . . working in an office . . . taking a cake to a neighbour . . . making music . . . smiling at someone unpleasant every time your path crosses theirs . . . writing an e-mail . . . taking a class . . .

composing a poem. It doesn't have to be anything amazing and spectacular from your perspective. You never know where it may be leading you, or what God might be preparing you for through it.

Call to mind now whatever it is.

Are you still true to your calling? Or have you listened to any lies or self-doubt?

Spend a moment dwelling in the Divine Presence contemplating these things. Listen to God's voice within your inner being. Take that voice seriously. Do not listen to any other voice.

Trust dreams. Trust your heart,

and trust your story.

Neil Gaiman

2
Ashes and Ravens

In the shadow of the castle of King Dw'i lay a village, and at the edge of the village, by the castle wall, was the house owned by the local blacksmith. Although he was the best blacksmith for a great distance, he was also a renowned drunkard and gambler. His wife and child often went hungry because he had no money left to buy food.

Recently, his wife had died and left him alone with their young daughter. People said he had beaten both his wife and daughter and that this was the cause of his wife's death, but nothing could be proven. His daughter, Cariad, was a timid child who cowered at her father's presence.

One day, three men knocked at the black-smith's door, demanding payment for a loan. The

blacksmith had spent all his money on drink and
gambling, and so he offered the men his little
daughter instead. The men took Cariad as payment and gave her to their master Neidr.

Life with Neidr was worse for Cariad than life
with her father. He treated her with more con-
tempt and even harder fists than her father ever
had.

A short time later, the blacksmith's dead body
was found behind the local tavern. Since he had
died with more unpaid debts to Neidr, Neidr
claimed the blacksmith's house as his own, and so
Cariad found herself back in the place of her terrible childhood. The only thing different was that
now Neidr mistreated her instead of her father.

One day when Cariad was down at the well
getting water, she heard a great commotion. She
followed a crowd as they raced towards a pillar

of billowing smoke coming from the edge of the village. As she ran, she realised it was her house that was ablaze. The fire was so intense that no one could get close enough to it to throw water on the flames.

When the fire had burned out, the villagers went in the wreckage and found Neidr's body in the midst of the ashes. He had been trying to work the blacksmith's furnace when the house caught fire.

Cariad, finding herself homeless with no one to care for her, said, "What is to happen to me now?"

No one had an answer for her. All the villagers started to walk away.

"Wait!" cried Cariad. "What am I to do? Where shall I go?"

No one answered. They just kept walking away. But then Cariad heard a voice speaking behind her.

"Some say that King Dw'i will adopt those who ask him."

Cariad turned around to see who was talking. She saw a man in a long hooded cloak holding a walking staff with which he was poking around in the ashes of the house.

"What did you say?" asked Cariad

"Ask at the gate, child." The man pointed with his stick at the castle entrance.

Cariad looked at the drawbridge and great gate. Then she turned back to the man. "But what do I say?" she asked, but there was no one there. The man had gone.

Cariad looked for a moment longer at the pile of ash that had once been her house, and then she walked towards the castle gate. When she got there, the guards looked at her and smiled. Their shapes shone so brightly that Cariad's eyes were dazzled. They held glittering swords, their points resting on the ground, that were taller than she was.

"I've come to see King Dw'i," Cariad said nervously, "to ask to be adopted. I have no one. My father, now dead, sold me, and my master is now dead also, burned to death by his own hand, taking my house to ashes with him."

The guards continued to smile at Cariad. Cariad did not know how to take this, as she could not remember being smiled at before. There was a vague picture in the back of her mind of her mother smiling down at her when she was a small baby, but it was not a memory she could see clearly.

Just when Cariad thought that she was going to get nowhere, the great gate opened. The guards, continuing to smile, motioned for her to go in.

Once inside, a short man with a tall hat met Cariad. "Come with me, child," he said.

Cariad followed him into the great hall where King Dw'i sat at the far end on his throne. The short man led Cariad to the king and then stepped aside.

"So, you want to be adopted into my family, do you?" King Dw'i said.

"Yes please," said Cariad. "I have no one and nowhere to live."

"I know," said the king. "I have always been watching over you ever since you were born. Remember the time when you were lost in the woods and feared your father's hand for being late?"

"I do," said Cariad

"It was I who led you back. And oftentimes I told your father to treat you better, but he would not listen to my words. But sometimes I would cause him to fall asleep so that he did not harm you or your mother."

"How did you do that?" asked Cariad.

"I have my ways," said the king. "Now, go with Taran, and he will welcome you into my family. We have been waiting for you."

Cariad loved being a part of King Dw'i's family. She had no fear, and everyone in the castle smiled at her.

But every day she would go out the back door of the castle and down to the ash heap ruins of her old house. Each time, she found two great black ravens perched on the burned frame of the front door. When Cariad looked at the ravens, she saw them as her father and Neidr, there to taunt her as they croaked and screeched. She would walk around the rooms of the burned-down house, stirring the ashes and remembering all the harm and hurt that had been inflicted upon her. Every day she would go back again, bringing food to feed the ravens.

"You must love this place," said a voice behind her one day. "I have watched you come here so many times."

Cariad turned to see the man in the long hooded cloak with the walking staff, the same man she had seen the day her house burned down.

"Oh no," said Cariad. "I hate it here! The memories are painful and horrible. But I have to come back here. I have to feed the ravens and stir the ash."

"Why?" asked the man. "Why do you need to do those things?"

"The ravens taunt me," said Cariad. "Even when I am in the castle I see them from my window and hear them when I play in the grounds. I have to come back and feed them."

"Child," said the man, "King Dw'i has authority over the whole of this kingdom, including the ravens and even the ashes. You are a child of the king now—and you can use that position to command the ravens to go, and they will have to go. You do not have to walk in the ashes anymore. Unless you want to. It's your choice."

"But the birds will not listen to me," said Cariad. "I have tried before to get rid of them, and they won't go."

"Use the authority that is now in you as a child of the king," said the man. "Command them to go."

Cariad looked at the ravens croaking at her louder than she had ever heard them. "Go away!" she said, but the birds screeched even louder. They seemed almost to laugh at her.

Cariad closed her eyes and said to herself, "I am a child of King Dw'i. I have the authority." She looked back at the ravens, and this time she saw the truth. With command in her voice, she said, "Go away! You have no right to ruin my life and keep causing me pain! Be gone and don't ever come back!"

The ravens turned and flew up over the trees and away across the woods.

As Cariad turned with a smile, she saw King Dw'i coming up the path.

"I was wondering how long it would take you to get rid of those ravens," said the king. "Now, what about this ash heap then? Shall we plough it over?"

Cariad looked at the ashes. "No," she said, "an empty patch of ground would still remind me of my time here. Could you make it into a garden for me instead? With beautiful flowers and a peaceful pool where I could sit with you and build good memories?"

"A place of beauty from ashes," said the king. "I like that. It will be done."

For many years after, Cariad often sat with King Dw'i in the garden. The ravens never returned, and Cariad's heart healed well as she grew up, a well-loved child of the king.

Reflection

We all have experienced hard, bleak times, some of us more so than others. Those painful times can cast long dark shadows over the rest of our lives. This story, however, affirms that we have a Greater Power interacting with our lives, one that is stronger than our hurtful memories. We can go, at any time, to this Greater Power with confidence, since unconditional love is flowing from it to us. This is what the scripture means in Hebrews 4:16: "So let us come boldly to the throne of our gracious God. There we will receive mercy and find grace to help us when we need it most" (NLT). Like Cariad, we not only have the power to dwell in safety now, but we also have the inner authority to create something new and beautiful out of the ashes and devastation of the past.

Meditation

Without becoming overwhelmed or going too deeply into the memories, draw to mind all the hurts that still affect your inner self, all the old events and circumstances that continue to cause you pain. Now allow the Divine Presence to seep into your heart, into your inner being, and overwhelm these things in your mind. Allow the flow of the Spirit to flood these negative things and wash them away.

Now meditate for a few moments on the words from this paraphrase of Philippians 4:6–7:

Don't let these negative, hurtful things affect you anymore. Instead, bring them to God. Tell God about them and leave them in the Divine Hand. Thank God for all the good things. Then you will experience God's deep peace, which is beyond anything we can understand.

This peace will guard your heart and your mind as you live in Christ Jesus.

Now dwell on this paraphrase of the verse that follows, Philippians 4:8:

Plant flowers of things that are true, of things that are noble, things that are just, things that are pure, things that are lovely, things of good report, things of virtue and anything praiseworthy, and then meditate on these things.

The painful past cannot be undone—but it *can* become fertile ground for new growth. What are some "flowers" that you would like to plant in your life? What action can you take to begin your garden?

Now imagine for a few moments that your inner being is a garden. Picture each blossom and leaf. Let the stream of living water flow through it, welling up to eternal life (John 4:14).

Times of depression [may] tell you
that it's either time to get out
of the story you're in
and move into a new story,
or that you're in the right story
but there's some piece of it
you are not living out.
Carol S. Pearson

Even your pain can become a garden,

a garden of compassion.

Keep your heart open;

let sorrow plant seeds

of love and of wisdom.

Rumi

3
Bags of Stones

Once there were three travelling companions on the path of life, Skellig, Cariad, and Dern. As they travelled, they came across a man on the road wearing a hooded cloak and holding a walking staff.

"You will need these," said the man and held out three bags to the three companions.

Skellig and Cariad took a bag each and threw the straps over their shoulders. Dern, however, did not take a bag. Instead, he stepped around the man so he could go on his way.

"You will need this," the man said, "if you are to enter the garden."

"I have heard of this garden," said Dern, "but I am not a believer in it. I shall walk my own way and I will not need a bag."

"Very well," said the man. "So be it."

At that, the man disappeared, and the three companions walked on.

"Why did you take those bags?" jeered Dern. "They will just get in the way."

"They are necessary to get into the garden," said Cariad. "You were a fool not to take yours."

Dern shook his head and walked on.

Not far from where they had met the man they came to a fork in the road. A man with a sword in his hand stood at the divide. When they approached him, he stopped them.

"Those with bags go down that path." He pointed to his right. "Those with no bags down that path." He pointed to his left. When he saw that Dern had no bag, he said, "You may take a bag from me if you wish. I have extras."

Skellig and Cariad urged Dern to take a bag. Dern let out a frustrated sigh and walked off down the path to the man's left, shaking his head.

Skellig and Cariad, saddened to have lost Dern, went down the path to the man's right.

Dern continued in the sun for some time, and though feeling sad to have lost the companionship of Skellig and Cariad, he felt happy that he was walking in his own way. The path before him was smooth and flat and had many nice things to eat on the bushes and trees that grew on either side. He walked on quite content with his journey, until he got to a small town.

At the town gate, Dern was directed to the tavern, where he was told there were rooms for him to stay.

As Dern walked to the tavern, he passed some beggars on the roadside who held out their hands to him. Dern turned his face away and continued on to the tavern. "After all," he said to himself, "I have nothing with me to give them."

Once in the tavern, he was offered a room and something to eat and drink. This would be paid for, he was told, at the end of his journey.

Dern enjoyed his meal and got on well with the others in the tavern who also seemed to be enjoying life without a bag.

As Dern went to his room, he saw some people at the doorway taking bags from a traveller in a hooded cloak with a walking staff.

"That stupid man," Dern thought to himself. "Will he never give up? Why is he so determined to give us something we clearly don't need?"

As Dern passed the man, the man held out a bag and said, "You will need this on your journey to get into the garden."

Dern turned away and went to his room for the night.

The next morning as Skellig and Cariad arose from their sleep on the roadside, they noticed something in their bags that hadn't been there before.

"What are these?" Cariad asked, pulling out a stone that filled her hand.

"Stones," replied Skellig. "I have some too. Where did they come from?" He took one of the stones and went to throw it into the river.

"Don't do that," said a voice.

Skellig and Cariad turned to see the man who had given them the bags in the first place.

"Why not?" asked Skellig

"Keep them in your bag," the man replied, "until you reach the garden."

Skellig and Cariad looked at one another, and then back to the man. "What for?" asked Skellig. "They are heavy and will weigh us down." But even as Skellig spoke, the man was gone.

As Skellig and Cariad walked on into the morning, they came across a woman carrying a heavy load on her shoulders

"Can we help you with that?" Cariad and Skellig asked.

"Thank you," said the woman.

Skellig and Cariad took some of the load each and walked with the woman to a small cottage near by.

"Thank you," the woman said again and went into the house.

As Skellig and Cariad walked on, Skellig thought his bag seemed heavier. He reached into his bag and felt around. He was sure that this morning there were three stones in his bag, but now there seemed to be five.

Skellig turned to Cariad. "How many stones do you have in your bag?"

"Three," Cariad replied.

"Reach in and see," said Skellig.

Cariad reached into her bag and felt five stones. "That's strange," she said. "I wonder where the other two came from."

Skellig and Cariad walked on through the day. The path was not always easy, but they managed to travel it, and the scenery was beautiful. Along the way, they found people who needed their help, and they always gave it.

Meanwhile, Dern was feeling quite pleased with himself as he walked in the sunshine. The path was wide and easy, and he could not help feeling sorry for his foolish companions who had taken a bag.

"What did they think?" he said to himself. "Count on it, those bags will be filled with something along the way. But I have nothing to weigh me down or hinder me. I can walk on as I please."

Dern continued on the road all that day, while Skellig and Cariad had been walking all day up slopes and down rocky paths. Eventually, they saw a town in the distance.

"This bag is getting heavy," said Skellig. "I'm beginning to wish I hadn't taken it."

"And I seem to have a lot more stones now than before," said Cariad. "They just seem to appear in the bag."

"I've noticed something," said Skellig. "Remember that woman we helped this morning?"

"Yes," replied Cariad.

"Well, two stones appeared after she left us," said Skellig. "And those men the night before, the beggars? The first three stones appeared after we helped them. And now, as we have helped a few other people along the path today, our bags are filling with stones."

"What are you saying?" asked Cariad. "That stones appear in our bags when we help people?"

"That seems to be the case," said Skellig. "Maybe Dern had the right idea after all."

"Don't say that!" said Cariad. "There must be a reason for it, there must be a purpose."

"We'll see," said Skellig as they entered the town.

The man at the town gate directed them to the tavern where they had something to eat and drink and then settled down for the night.

The next day, as they rose and travelled on they came across a wounded deer. Cariad bent down to tend it, but Skellig kept walking.

"Leave it," he said over his shoulder. "It's just an animal."

But Cariad washed the deer's wound and then ripped her shirt and bandaged the hurt leg. As the deer hobbled off, Cariad felt her bag get heavier. She looked inside and found that more stones had appeared.

"You see?" said Skellig. "Whenever you do good, stones appear in your bag".

As Skellig and Cariad travelled on, Skellig was more discerning in whom he helped. He was not going to laden himself with stones from helping just any old person or sick and injured animals. But Cariad helped anyone and everything that she came across for the entire journey.

Much time passed, and one day as Skellig and Cariad walked out of a wood into a meadow, they saw Dern a short distance away.

"Dern!" shouted Cariad

Dern turned and walked over to Skellig and Cariad.

"Well, well," he said. "Look at you two, laden down with those bags! Been a hard walk, has it?"

"It's not been easy," said Cariad, "but I would say it has been worth it."

"Well, my walk has been easy and a lot of fun!" said Dern.

"Oh, we've had some good fun too," said Skellig, "and met some amazing people."

After the three companions had walked on together for a short time, they saw a man at the side of the road in a long hooded cloak holding a walking staff.

"Would you like a bag?" he asked Dern. "Even with an empty bag you can enter the garden. This is the last opportunity you will have to take a bag."

Dern shrugged. "I've told you before," he said. "I am not a believer in this garden."

Even though Skellig and Cariad tried to persuade Dern to take a bag, he would not. "There's no point" he said.

"This way then," said the man, pointing towards a tall wall with a large gate in it.

The three companions walked on, while the man went off back into the woods. Skellig, Cariad, and Dern reached a large gate. It bore a notice that said:

> *Welcome all who enter here.*
> *The garden filled with joy and cheer.*

Skellig and Cariad looked at one another.

"We made it!" said Skellig.

"Well," said Dern, "so the garden *is* real."

As he was saying this, the gate opened up before them, and there standing at the gate was the most magnificent person they had ever seen. He seemed to shine, and the sense of peace that flowed out from him was overwhelming.

"Welcome!" he said. "May I see your bags?"

Skellig and Cariad showed the man their bags, and he motioned for them to go past him.

Dern walked up to the man. "May I see your bag?" the man said.

"I don't have one," replied Dern.

"I see," said the man. "Then you must go through that door." The man pointed down the hill towards the end of the wall at a dark overgrown area. Dern looked in the direction the man was pointing. He looked back at Skellig and Cariad. With a sadness in his heart, he left his companions and walked in the direction the man had pointed.

"Now," the man said to Skellig and Cariad, "won't you please come in?"

In the garden, Skellig and Cariad looked around in wonder at all the incredible things that were there. The smells and the sights were far beyond anything they had ever experienced on their path, and a sense of joy and peace filled the air.

"May I have your bags?" said a voice.

Skellig and Cariad turned to see the traveller standing there in his hooded cloak, walking staff in hand. They handed their bags over to him.

"Hmm," the man said to Cariad. "Your bag is quite a lot heavier than the other one."

"Yes," said Skellig in his defence. "I noticed that whenever we did something good, the bags got heavier with stones. I didn't think it was fair to become laden down with a heavier burden when I was doing good, so I was more discerning in whom I helped and what I did."

"I see," said the man. "Well, come with me." He led them to a hall with a great table in the centre. He tipped out Skellig's bag at one end and Cariad's bag out at the other, but instead of stones tumbling out of the bag, great jewels came rolling out—rubies and sapphires, diamonds and jade, and all sorts of other jewels.

"So," said the man, "these are the treasures you each gained on the path of life. They are yours now for all eternity."

Reflection

Our choices in this life have lasting consequences. Our actions matter, and even the smallest acts of kindness have enduring effects, even into eternity. This world has impact on the world to come—or perhaps, as the Celts believed, the visible world and the invisible world are not so separate as we sometimes think. Whatever is done in one spills over into the other in ways we can't perceive until we've crossed over.

Meditation

As you walk life's path, how do you act? What is it that drives your heart? Is your priority to make things less difficult for yourself? Or is helping others a higher priority?

Is there a "stone" that you've resisted carrying—some action that would help another but would make your own life more difficult?

In Luke 6:45 Jesus tells us that out of the overflow of the heart the mouth speaks. His statement suggests a scenario where someone knocks over a jar that's full to the brim. What comes out will be whatever was inside the jar. In our case, often our words and actions are not so much the results of thought-out decisions as they are our inner selves flowing out before cognitive control can take over.

What is your heart full of? What would "overflow" if the "jar" of your inner being was knocked over? How do the contents of your inner being relate to the message of this story?

Spend time dwelling on these ideas. Then rest in God wordlessly, with no thought of "should" or "ought." At the end of this time, what comes to mind? Is there any "stone" you have refused to carry? Any bag you've refused to fill? If so, why? Can you release your unwillingness into the Divine Hand?

Make compassion a daily thing,
not an extraordinary thing
but the thing you do instantly, immediately,
as soon as you perceive another's need.
They say by doing so
you'll lay up treasure in heaven.
I think that means you'll make the universe—
all that IS, the entire reality—
a richer thing.
You create "heart wealth,"
something far deeper
than any visible riches
we could imagine.
Ann T. Furstow

What story do you want to tell?

A narrow, miserly, little story?

Or a story of such width and depth

that it spills over

onto everyone around you?

You choose!

Ramon Casas

4

Parable of the Prisoner

There was once a man who was being held in prison. He was chained at his wrists and his ankles, and the shackles were so tight they had drawn blood.

The prison cell in which he was kept was below ground level, so there was no natural light; in fact, there was no light at all, making the place so dark that he could not see his hand in front of his face. The man spent his entire life with his eyes closed, slumped in a corner, feeling the ache of the shackles on his wrists and ankles.

One day someone came to the prison governor and told him he had to let this man go.

"But he is under the death sentence," the prison governor said.

As it turned out, though, the punishment had been cancelled, and someone had paid all the man's debts. The man could go free.

Reluctantly, the prison governor unlocked the doors and unshackled the prisoner, giving him over to the man who had come for him.

The prisoner, now a free man, was led out of the prison into the light of the world. He was dazzled by the light and the world around him. It would take some getting used to, being free and living in the light.

The man struggled with his new life. He worried that there had to be more to it than simply being made free. The life he was now living was completely alien to him. It had no real connection with his life inside the prison. He had been there so long that he was not used to having freedom in his heart and light in his life.

To make things worse, the prison governor, annoyed that he had lost a prisoner he still believed to be guilty, found ways to whisper into the man's ear that he wasn't really free. "You are still bound," he hissed. "Can't you feel the shackles cutting into your wrists and ankles? Face reality, man! You are still a prisoner."

Eventually, the man gave in to the whispers. He slumped down in a dark alleyway. His eyes fell shut, and he felt the pain in his wrists and ankles. He knew the prison governor was right—he was still a prisoner.

The man went back to living in the dark. With his eyes closed, he saw only darkness. He felt the weight of the shackles around his arms and legs. He hung his head and accepted that he was a prisoner.

Meanwhile, the sun was shining above his head. People were calling and laughing in the next street. The smells of cooking filled the air, along with the sweet scents of fresh grass and summer flowers.

There was an entire world of light the man could have explored.

But he didn't. In his heart, he was still a prisoner—and in his mind, he had created prison walls and tight shackles that were as cold and harsh as those he had known before. He was truly bound and chained.

REFLECTION

Although this is the shortest of the four tales, it may well be the most important. Many times, we all live as though we are still in bondage to the darkness of the past. We are shackled by a lie.

The Christian scriptures promise that we can find freedom in the Divine Presence (2 Corinthians 3:17). In the Gospel of John, Jesus says, speaking of himself, "If the Son sets you free you will be free indeed" (8:36 NIV). Yet despite these statements, even "religious" people often live lives that are restricted by their inner prisons. They believe a lie about themselves—and that lie is as dark and narrow a cell as any prison could hold.

MEDITATION

Sometimes, we may need help from others to let go of our inner bondage. We may need to talk with a trusted friend or a professional counsellor. But one of the best things we can do for ourselves is to replace the lies in our heads with truth. Here is one way to do that.

Read these three verses:

Now the real authority is the Spirit, the Wind of I Am that breathes through the Universe. Wherever that Wind blows, it removes all barriers and limitations. (2 Corinthians 3:17, *Strong's Greek Lexicon*)

If the Son sets you free, you are truly free. (John 8:36 NLT)

It was for freedom that Christ set us free; therefore keep standing firm and do not be subject again to a yoke of slavery. (Galatians 5:6 NAS)

Read them over and over, in the styles of Lectio Divina. (See page 88 for instructions for this ancient spiritual practice.)

If you keep telling the same sad small story, you

will keep living the same sad small life.

Jean Houston

LECTIO DIVINA

"Lectio Divina" is a Latin term that means "divine reading." It's a way of reading the scriptures whereby we gradually let go of our own agendas and open ourselves to what God wants to say to us. The practice of Lectio Divina can be separated into five parts: read, reflect, respond, rest, relate.

READ

Set aside time each day to read scripture, but during this time don't be concerned about volume. In other words, don't say to yourself, "Today I will read three chapters"—or two chapters or even one chapter. Instead, slowly begin reading a scripture passage, savouring each word and phrase. Read until you notice a word or phrase that jumps out at you. This word or phrase will touch something in you; it will resonate with you or attract you in some way. It may even disturb you. When this happens, don't read any further. Read and reread the same sentence or verse. Come back to it again on the following day, and maybe even for several days. Stay with it.

REFLECT

Think about what this passage is saying to you. Ponder the word or phrase. Be like Mary who treasured God's words to her and pondered them in her heart (Luke 2:19). Let the scripture word or phrase sink deeper and deeper, through all the layers of your thoughts. Allow God to speak to you through it. Listen for what this scripture says to you within the circumstances of your current life. Don't think in abstracts or concern yourself with doctrine and theology. (There is a time and place for that, but this is not it). What gifts does this passage offer you? What insights rise to the surface of your heart? What does it demand of you?

RESPOND

The Benedictines refer to this step as *oratio*: prayer. In other words, express what is within your heart in words of thanksgiving . . . or petition; praise . . . or lament. Be honest with God. You may want to respond aloud, or you may want to speak silently to God within your mind. You might want to write down your thoughts. If you linger with the same Bible passage for several days, recording your responses each day in a journal, when you look back you may be surprised how many different things came out of your heart in response to the same word or phrase.

REST

At the end of your meditation, let go of all your thoughts. Surrender even the words themselves upon which you have been meditating. Allow yourself to rest silently in God's love and peace. A mother holding her sleeping baby doesn't need to speak to communicate her love, nor do lovers need to fill every moment with chatter in order to commune with each other. This is the same sort of moment between you and God, a moment of intimacy and total trust.

RELATE

It is no good reading the Bible, even if God speaks to you through it, if you do not relate it to the way you live your life. We're not talking here about applying religious rules to your life or trying to "be good." Instead, take the particular passage of scripture with you throughout the day. Allow it to continue to work in your mind and heart. When you take a "me moment," think back to the word or phrase. See how it applies to the daily circumstances of your life. Allow it to weave through the hours of your everyday life.

Stories can make the heart bigger.

Ben Okri

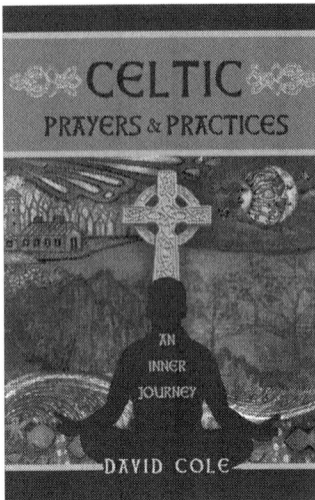

Celtic Prayers & Practices
An Inner Journey

Author: David Cole
Price: US $14.95
Paperback
E-book Available
ISBN: 978-1-625241-03-0

A Celtic Pilgrimage into the Center of Your Being

If you long to set out on an inner journey, this book is a guide to point you in the right direction. Its simple and practical prayer techniques from Celtic and other ancient traditions make use of your breath, Nature, scripture, and prayer words. Just as the Celts set out on long voyages of discovery, you will find the road that leads you to spiritual adventure—and the Image of God that is the light within your heart.

The kingdom of heaven can be reached from any land.
    —***Saint Samthann*** (8th-century Irish abbess)

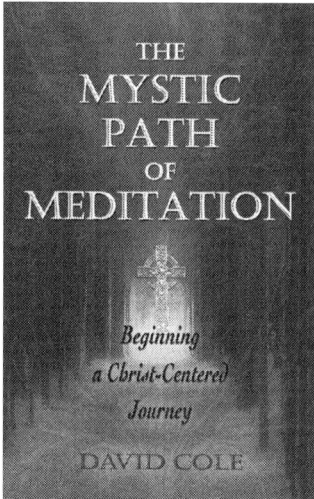

The Mystic Path of Meditation: Beginning a Christ-Centered Journey

Author: David Cole
Price: US $14.95
Paperback
E-book Available
154 pages
ISBN: 978-1-937211-99-8

Explore the Christian theology that underpins meditation—and discover the practical spiritual benefits of this ancient practice.

"Meditation is one of the great treasures of our Christian contemplative tradition, though largely forgotten by modern churches. In this delightful book, David Cole gently invites readers to rediscover this ancient path to deeper relationship with God. David writes with a spirit of ease and joy as he guides us through meditation with scripture, our breath, our bodies, and the natural world. This insightful and accessible book is a welcome addition to the contemplative renewal of our time."

— **_Mark Kutolowski_**, OblSB, Salva Terra peace pilgrim and founder of New Creation Wilderness Programs

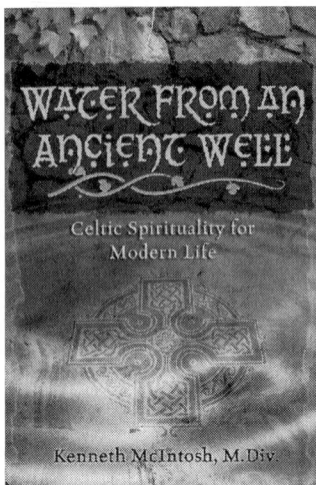

Water from an Ancient Well: Celtic Spirituality for Modern Life

Author: Kenneth McIntosh, M.Div.

Price: $24.95

Paperback

E-book Available

352 pages

ISBN: 978-1-933630-98-4

Discover the world of the ancient Celtic Christians and find practical insights for living in the twenty-first century.

"When I was reading *Water from an Ancient Well*, I sometimes felt like I taking a spiritual pilgrimage to Cano Cristales, the most beautiful river in the world or the river of five colors. Located near the town of La Macarena in Colombia, South America, the river is famous for its colorful blotches of blue, green, black, and red causing some to call it the river that ran away to paradise. If you want to run away to paradise for a couple of days, and drink living water from a source unlike any other, read Kenneth McIntosh's deeply satisfying book."

—***Leonard Sweet***, best-selling author and professor.

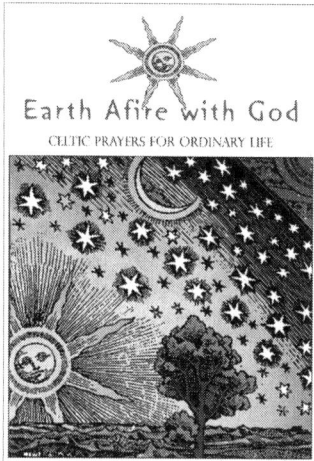

Earth Afire with God: Celtic Prayers for Ordinary Life

Author: Anamchara Books
Price: $12.95
Paperback
E-book Available
120 pages
ISBN: 978-1-933630-96-0

Here are prayers and blessings to sanctify your daily life. They will remind you to look for the holiness of the everyday; they will show you the real presence of God in Creation. Illumine your life with the ancient Celts' perspective on prayer. Each glimpse we have of the Earth's beauty, each ordinary sound we hear, every bite of food we eat, and even our daily routines, can all reveal God.

Kenneth McIntosh, author of *Water from an Ancient Well, Celtic Spirituality for Modern Life*, writes, "This book knocks the dust off ancient treasures—such as selections from the *Carmina Gadelica*—and also introduces some lovely new prayers, all written from the Celtic perspective."

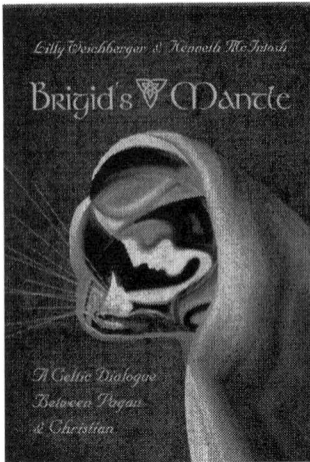

**Brigid's Mantle:
A Celtic Dialogue
Between Pagan
and Christian**
Author: Lilly Weichberger
and Kenneth McIntosh
Price: $14.95
Paperback
E-book Available
ISBN: 978-1-62524-262-4

Long ago, the story goes, Brigid flung out her mantle over the world. Beneath its shelter, the Earth and its people could find healing, insight, and growth. This legend, shared by both Celtic Pagans and Celtic Christians, makes the point that a mantle is not a box, a small rigid container meant to keep some things inside while excluding others. Instead, a mantle is wide, flexible, inclusive. Using this as their central metaphor, the authors—one a Pagan healer and the other a Christian minister—engage in a dialogue that is ultimately about what it means to be spiritual, to be a person of faith. With Brigid, as both a Pagan Goddess and a Christian saint, at the center of their dialogue, the authors first provide the historical foundation for the Celtic culture, past and present. They build on this a concept of Celtic spirituality that embraces the arts, Nature, the supernatural world, compassion for those in need, and gender equality.

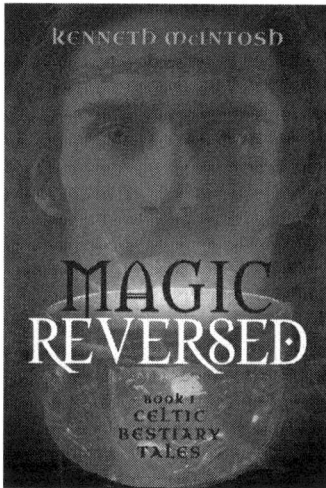

Magic Reversed
Author: Kenneth McIntosh
Price: $17.95
Paperback
E-book Available
ISBN: 978-1-62524-240-2

This book can be enjoyed on several levels. It's an action-packed young adult fantasy, brimming with adventure, danger, and romance. Young adult readers will relate to the tension between Finn and Freya that slowly blossoms into something deeper. Fantasy-lovers of all ages will be delighted to encounter characters from Celtic mythology: the wizard Merlin, the Goddess Brigid, and the ravenous walking dead spawned by the Dark Lord's cauldron. At the same time, those who are attracted to Celtic spirituality will find strands of symbolism, like gold threads in an ancient tapestry, meshed unobtrusively with this tale of a young hero's journey to save his world.

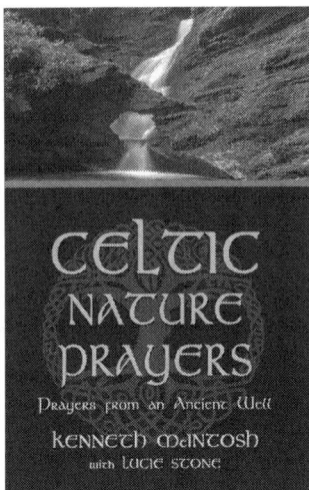

Celtic Nature Prayers:
Prayers from an Ancient Well
Author: Kenneth McIntosh,
compiled by Lucie Stone
Price: $14.95
Paperback
ISBN: 978-1-62524-263-1

Commune with God in nature using these ancient and modern prayers, with additional text written by Kenneth McIntosh, author of the bestselling *Water from an Ancient Well: Celtic Spirituality for Modern Life*. The Celts found the Divine in every tree and blade of grass, and we too can be refreshed and enriched by this primal love for the Earth. This prayerbook offers a Nature-focused collection based on ancient Celtic prayers, weaving together words of hope, worship, and challenge. Each prayer is an opportunity to connect our personal faith with the Earth we share.

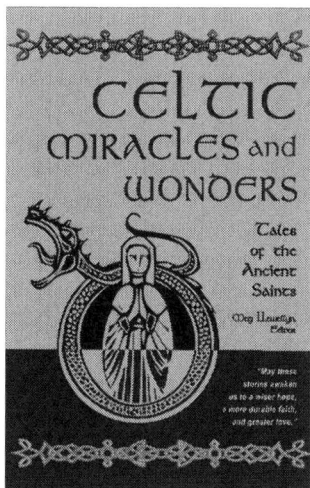

Celtic Miracles and Wonders:
Tales of the Ancient Saints
Editor: Meg Llewellyn
Price: $17.95
Paperback
ISBN: 978-1-62524-275-4

These are stories of the ancient Celtic saints—of Patrick and Brigit, Columcille and many others—in the words and cadences used by ordinary people who were alive during the nineteenth and early twentieth centuries. Other accounts of these saints' lives may be more historically accurate, but those contained here tell us as much about the people who told the stories as they do about the ancient saints: they show us those saints' legacy lived out in people's lives and imaginations more than a thousand years later. These tales reveal an ongoing conviction that the invisible world is as real as the visible one. They show us human beings living in constant, tangible friendship with God, with the supernatural, and with animals. And they lead us into a world where holiness and the imagination have joined hands, a world where we can truly catch glimpses of miracles and wonders.

Anamchara Books

Books to Inspire
Your Spiritual Journey

In Celtic Christianity, an *anamchara* is a soul friend, a companion and mentor (often across the miles and the years) on the spiritual journey. Soul friendship entails a commitment to both accept and challenge, to reach across all divisions in a search for the wisdom and truth at the heart of our lives.

At Anamchara Books, we are committed to creating a community of soul friends by publishing books that lead us into deeper relationships with God, the Earth, and each other. These books connect us with the great mystics of the past, as well as with more modern spiritual thinkers. They are designed to build bridges, shaping an inclusive spirituality where we all can grow.

To find out more about Anamchara Books and order our books, visit **www.AnamcharaBooks.com** today.

Anamchara Books
Vestal, New York 13850
www.AnamcharaBooks.com

Made in the USA
Middletown, DE
13 August 2017